The Elements of Short Fiction
A Practical Guide for Writers

by
Jennifer Gessner

Copyright © 2025 by Jennifer Gessner

Published by Frontlist Editorial Services
Sleepy Hollow, NY 10591

All rights reserved. No part of this publication may be reproduced, distributed, or transmitted in any form or by any means, including photocopying, recording, or other electronic or mechanical methods, without the prior written permission of the publisher, except in the case of brief quotations embodied in critical reviews and certain other noncommercial uses permitted by copyright law. For permission requests, contact the author at jennifergessner@frontlisteditorial.com.

ISBN: 978-1-890586-88-1

Book cover and interior design: Tara Framer Design
Publishing services: Robert Kern, TIPS Publishing Services, Carrboro, NC
Printer: Minuteman Press of East Haven, CT

Printed in the United States of America

First edition January 2025

29 28 27 26 25   5 4 3 2 1

There are two men inside the artist,
the poet and the craftsman.
One is born a poet.
One becomes a craftsman.

~ Emile Zola

MORE ACCLAIM FOR
THE ELEMENTS OF SHORT FICTION

"You know how most how-to books could be condensed to a third of their length? In *The Elements of Short Fiction: A Practical Guide for Writers*, Jennifer Gessner has done just that. In engaging, pragmatic language, Gessner reassures readers—and teachers—that anyone can learn the craft of writing. 'If your muse is not waiting for you, craft will always be there.' Peppered with personal anecdotes and annotated examples, this gem of a writer's guide earns its place on the bookshelf next to *Bird by Bird* and *The Elements of Style*."

~ Daphne Uviller, author of *This Was Not the Plan* and *Super in the City*

"I've been using the 'Gessner Method' in my classes for the past 14 years, and I can confidently say—it works. For writers just starting out, these ten elements offer both guidance and a gentle push to focus on language and craft. At the same time, they serve as a valuable reminder for more experienced writers to return to the core principles of strong storytelling. If you are a writer or a teacher of writing, you will find these elements useful."

~ Jeffrey Becker, author and professor of Creative Writing

I could not have created this book without the guidance of my friend and a mentor in the teaching of Creative Writing, Esteban Martinez. He created much of the framework for the elements and helped me to discover my own talents for teaching the craft of writing.

ACKNOWLEDGMENTS

Writing a book is hard - even if it's your thing. Maybe especially if it's your thing. And it doesn't happen in a vacuum. While the bulk of the creative work happens alone with your thoughts, the actual making of the book is a team effort.

Many folks played a part in the publication of this book, and I'd like to acknowledge a few people in particular.

Amy Baldwin was an early and multi-time reader of my manuscript. Thank you for your astute suggestions for improvement and for never wavering in your fierce support and consummate cheerleading of my work.

Tara Framer devoted her time and creativity to designing a lovely, captivating book. Thank you for your dedication to the pursuit of perfection and for always aiming for excellence.

David Kellogg's steadfast stewardship has imbued me with confidence. His insight on the business side of the publishing process has offered clarity. And he's delightful to boot. Thank you for your generous gift of time in mentoring me. It is one that will continue to give.

Steve Thomas, my former Department Chair, was the first to ask for my notes on how to teach "the Gessner Method," as he dubbed it. Thank you for inspiring me to write this book and for providing me one of the greatest accolades of my professional career.

To everyone who took the time to review my work and offer guidance, thank you for lending your thoughtful, trusted opinions. It means a great deal to me.

TABLE OF CONTENTS

PREFACE		xiii
CHAPTER 1	Specific Person, Place and Time Frame	1
CHAPTER 2	Active Language	6
CHAPTER 3	Objective Point of View	9
CHAPTER 4	Few Adverbs	14
CHAPTER 5	Five Senses	17
CHAPTER 6	Suspense	21
CHAPTER 7	Emotion	26
CHAPTER 8	Character Development	30
CHAPTER 9	Distorting the Truth	39
CHAPTER 10	Editing	42

APPENDICES

APPENDIX A	Stories that Model the Elements	50
APPENDIX B	Writing Workshop Guidelines	56
APPENDIX C	Pre-Writing Outline Template	59

WORKS CITED	61
ABOUT THE AUTHOR	63

*Learn the rules like a pro
so you can break them like an artist.*

~ Pablo Picasso

PREFACE

If you have... friends who aspire to become writers, the second greatest favor you can do... is to present them with copies of The Elements of Style. *The first greatest, of course, is to shoot them now, while they're happy.*

~ Dorothy Parker

The Elements of Style, by Strunk and White, is a tiny little book that has been the go-to guide for English teachers because it manages to condense the basic principles of English grammar in its mere 80 pages. This book, The Elements of Short Fiction, intends to teach the principles of writing a short story in a similar number of pages.

In the classroom, I teach how to write a short story using ten elements and these elements make up the tools for this craft. *Tools* and *craft* are the operative words here. I assure my students that writing is a skill like any other and can be learned. Some doubt this and many believe in the myth of the muse, of an innate influence that whispers only to the lucky few. This is no myth, though. Some people do seem to have a natural talent for writing: the born poet.

It might feel discouraging to read this, especially if you worry you're not a born poet. But consider the following two anecdotes. I'm the youngest in my family and desperately wanted to join my siblings in school before I was of age. Instead, I would carry out to the yard a TV Tray and chair, a pad of paper and pencil, and one of my parent's anthologies of Hans Christian Andersen stories. Not the picture books, but the text of his tales. I would then sit outside and transcribe my favorites. Now, I wasn't composing, as far as creating anything new, but I have to believe a couple of things: this transcription taught me something about syntax and structure and, moreover, that I was drawn to this at such a young age suggests I have an innate love of words and a talent for writing. This is backed up by how young I began speaking and reading, and also by writing awards I won as early as middle school.

Second anecdote: I studied classical piano for more than ten years. My teacher would enter me in several different annual statewide competitions. Some of these were in auditoriums with a bunch of other kids and some were in small rooms but all were, essentially, me playing alone in front of a panel of judges. Nerve wracking! The structure of these was such that if you earned the highest score, Superior, three years in a row, you won a trophy. If you got an Excellent (or lower) at any time along the way you were back to square one. Over seven years of competing, I earned two of these trophies — a great accomplishment. However, if someone wheeled a piano into the room I could noodle around but probably couldn't play any song all the way through. You see, I am not a natural musician. I love music, and have a good ear and sense of rhythm, but nothing else comes naturally to me. I just worked hard and practiced. In short, I learned the skill of piano playing and did so well enough to succeed.

When I began teaching Introduction to Creative Writing, I approached it from the same perspective. If one learns the basic structure of an activity — playing the piano, swinging a golf club, writing a short story — one can practice these skills over and over to success, even if one is not a natural musician, a natural athlete or a natural story teller. This idea of focusing on the craft rather than the theory of writing is practical and accessible to all, including beginning writers.

There will always be the true storytellers, those who entertain their friends with their latest adventure. This is the equivalent of playing an instrument by ear, and this person will come to creating fiction more naturally than someone who hasn't been telling stories most of her life. But anyone can learn the craft of storytelling through writing.

I've taught in this way for more than two decades so imagine my delight when one of the hottest writers backed me up. In several interviews, Taylor Swift, mega-superstar songstress who describes herself as a songwriter who sings rather than a singer who writes, has commented on her writing process. She shared that sometimes she wakes in the night and the whole song is right there, ready to record. She said she can't explain where this comes from, that it feels almost separate from her, as if she's just the vehicle. And then, other times, that mysticism is unattainable so she must rely on the craft of songwriting. So sometimes we're both the born poet and the craftsman. And if your muse is not waiting for you, craft will always be there.

A guiding principle for clear, captivating writing is to consider the structure of poetry. On the first day of class, I hold up two pieces of paper, one with a poem and one with prose. I ask the students, all sitting some distance away, to point to the poem. They're able to, of course, just as they're able to explain why it's so easy to identify. Poetry typically has short lines written vertically. We expect this disciplined writing from poetry, writing that is concise and precise. And poems evoke our emotions because of this discipline. Yet, this is just as important in prose. You want to use the exact word you mean and do so as simply as possible.

I prefer to use the short story format because it is a perfect work of fiction. It takes the concision and precision of a poem and the narrative flow of a novel and condenses them to a work of art. It is also less intimidating than a poem or a novel; more familiar than creative nonfiction. Yet the rules learned here, the ones that will help you craft a short story, can be applied to all disciplines of writing.

In an homage to Strunk & White — that they can teach the core of our complex grammatical structure in so few words — I thought I'd do the same for the writing of short fiction. This book is rising to a challenge: in fewer than 80 pages, teach a novice writer to create a meaningful, well developed, engaging work of short fiction.

Before beginning, allow me one caveat. I teach these elements of short fiction in a linear fashion because time is linear, but they work through layering and weaving together. Thus, creating any one of these elements often requires the aid of the others.

Let's start with the elements themselves. They're explained below and this list creates the table of contents:

1. **Specific Person, Place and Time Frame:** A story must revolve around a main character. This main character must be somewhere. This character's story must take place in some amount of time.

2. **Active Language:** Readers want to feel a part of the story, connecting with the characters, and engaged with the action. This cannot occur with the typical overuse of passive language. The quickest way to this active voice is to minimize if not nearly eliminate to-be verbs: Is, Am, Are, Was, Were, Be, Been, Being.

3. **Objective Point of View:** Beginning writers must learn to create a world for their readers by understanding the constructs of writing fiction. For the purposes of this book, we'll approach

point of view specifically from the objective rather than the omniscient.

4. **Few Adverbs:** If you've chosen the precise active verb (see Chapter 2), you needn't define it with an adverb. These weigh down and distract from the rigor of your description usually through redundancy.

5. **Five Senses:** Because you want your readers to feel wholly present in the scene of your story, you must tap into the means by which we take in any scene — either real or fiction. This is through our sense of sight, sound, taste, touch and smell. Create such a sensory experience for your readers and we'll linger, remembering the feel of your writing.

6. **Suspense:** This is a tricky one. Folks often think that suspense means car chases, psychological thrillers, horror films. Yet, in any good work of fiction, suspense is the single idea that grabs your attention and keeps you holding on throughout the 10 pages of a short story or the 900 of a long novel.

7. **Emotion:** This is a fun one. The first six elements focus on putting your readers in the room with your characters and letting them get to know these folks who've been roaming the rooms of your mind. The Emotion element is not about how the characters are feeling — that comes from your vivid sensory development (see Chapter 5). The Emotion element is about manipulating your readers' feelings and we do this through pacing.

8. **Character Development:** Simply put, good fiction is character driven. Yes, the story is important but not as important as who's living it. What your characters must be above all else is believable. To this end, they must seem real — even if a dog or a wizard. Thus, you must create characters who possess complexity, depth and humanity.

9. **Distorting of the Truth:** Fiction springs from the bounty of your imagination. No doubt it will be sprinkled with and likely even inspired by your real life, otherwise known as your best resource, but please don't transcribe your diary. This is fiction after all.

10. **Careful Editing:** For all of the elements that precede this one, editing is where the bulk of your work happens, for editing is the work of revision. Getting your story on paper or screen allows

you some clay to mold; editing forms that clay into a shape: a vase, a bowl, a cup, a horse, whatever you want, metaphorically. Without careful editing, you have nothing but the lump of clay.

Because these elements were developed and refined with my students over many years of teaching, this book is appropriate for an academic setting. However, I developed this method to allow anyone to learn to tell her or his story. Thus there are two audiences for this book.

If you are a teacher, you may create a lesson plan around each of the 10 elements or use the exercises provided at the end of each chapter. The basic structure is to ask students to write up to a three-page piece for each element, resulting in 10 separate works. Clarify that this will yield an incomplete story until all 10 elements are present. Each subsequent piece of writing will add on the remaining elements, one at a time, accumulatively. For example, the first assignment will focus on just the element of Specific Person, Place and Time Frame. The second assignment will include Specific Person, Place and Time Frame and will add Active Language. The third assignment will include Specific Person, Place and Time Frame, Active Language, and will add Objective Point of View. Etc. This repetition of the elements provides the practice needed to learn the craft.

Ask each student to read their narrative in front of the class as you, the teacher, lead the workshop. Much of the students' learning experience will come from hearing their story read and then hearing the audience's response. They will also learn much from model stories that demonstrate the use of the elements. You may use mine, found in Appendix A, or share ones you prefer, so long as they model the assignments.

For a three-credit course that meets twice a week, I typically take a full class period to give the assignment — explaining the element, how it works in a narrative, and dissecting a corresponding model story. Then the following three class periods are used to workshop, so two weeks for each assignment. In a 16-week course, the first assignment includes the first four elements. Because this is a writing class and not a literature course, the workshop should focus on the presence and correct use of the elements and not on any analysis of the story.

If you are an independent writer reading this book on your own, the exercises found at the end of each chapter and your analysis of the model stories will help you to create your short works. Each exercise teaches the process of the given element, and adding on to each one cumulatively will give you great practice in mastering them. You'll want to read and pick apart model stories to see how the author uses these elements. I have demonstrated how to do this with the model stories in Appendix A.

For both academic and independent writers, you'll find that you will not write a narrative piece until you reach the observation exercise in Chapter 5. The first four chapters set the stage for this initial writing exercise. And even this observation work in Chapter 5 will not yield a complete work of fiction as not all of the elements will be present. But, as you'll discover, it's easier to learn how to pay attention to details by recording something you've experienced rather than something you've imagined.

For both audiences, it's good to remember that this book is a beginner's guide to fiction intended to help writers to build their skills. It is neither the final word nor sole formula for great writing.

A word about the appendices. These provide ancillary information for you to further your work. As mentioned above:

- **Appendix A** has a collection of short fiction, each with a thorough analysis, that models what you are aiming for in your own writing. Permissions is a tricky business in the publishing world and I was not granted permission for all of the stories. For those stories for which I did receive permission (or they exist in the public domain), you'll find them annotated to show how they demonstrate the elements of good fiction. For the stories without permissions, you may find these via an Internet search using the title and author name.

- **Appendix B** contains the guidelines for a writing workshop. The workshop is integral for understanding your work and for growing as a writer. Indeed, it is the most essential aspect of improving writing and is the best part of a writing course. Over my many years, I think my students and I got this down to a harmonious science. These guidelines will work for both teachers and independent writers.

- **Appendix C** includes a template for how to draft a pre-writing outline.

CHAPTER 1

Specific Person, Place and Time Frame

If you write about everywhere you can end up writing about nowhere.
~ Salman Rushdie

No matter how many characters inhabit your story, one will be at its center. If you're itching to tell a story, no doubt you already have various characters milling around in your head, each giving you a piece of his or her own mind. If you're a novice writer, this may seem not only daunting but unnatural. Shouldn't someone who hears other voices seek mental health care? Perhaps. But she may just be a fiction writer. So, choose your main character with intention. This will be the one around whom the story revolves. The one whose journey will create the story.

Be sure to give this main character a name. When I was a kid, my dad and his best friend would get our families together for an excuse to do some elaborate cooking and eating. One year, a week before our gathering, dad's friend bought a lamb to butcher for one of these dinners. The kids named the lamb so, of course, their dad couldn't kill it and, instead, donated it to a farm where it ran free for the rest of its days and got regular visits. Names create identity, which, in turn, creates a connection. You'll read this many times throughout this guide: creating a connection between your readers and your characters, through which we learn something about the character and, thus, ourselves, is your principle goal as a writer.

Okay, now that we have our lead character, let's put her somewhere. The importance of setting cannot be underestimated. People behave differently in different environments. Think about how you act when sitting in a business meeting or a college classroom. Now consider your behavior when you're on the beach or at a nightclub. Different? I'm guessing for most of us it is vastly so.

The same is true for your characters. Do you envision her walking onto a balcony overlooking the French Riviera or surviving the urban grit of downtown LA? She'll have a different response for both. Make no mistake, your character's core self doesn't change, (though it should evolve/devolve; we'll get to this in Character Development) but she'll behave differently, perhaps with a different sense of propriety, depending on where you put her.

Another important aspect of setting is that it gives your readers a sense of place, grounding us. We like to know where we are so we can ready ourselves for our own expectations of that place. And if our protagonist behaves similarly or differently than we would in that same space, it will speak to her character and to our understanding of and connection with her.

When considering the time frame, remember that this does not mean the era of your story (the 1960s, the early aughts, medieval times), this is depicted through the setting. Rather, the time frame is the amount of time covered. Determine a sense of how long this snapshot of your character's life will last. Since this book instructs on the writing of short fiction it may not be much more than an hour. For example, you wouldn't write about your main character's high school career but, rather, you might focus on everything that happens in the last hour of her senior year, maybe her graduation ceremony. There are many novels that cover a great span of time. Some authors are masters of character development with stories that cover 30 years of the main character's life. For learning the process, keep your short stories — even those that fill 40 pages of text — to no more than 24 hours of your character's life.

To illustrate how this tight time frame works in short fiction, imagine you're at a concert and take a photo of the lead singer. Full of pride, you show your friends and they see the backs of many heads, a lot of lights and giant speakers, a big stage and, somewhere in the center, the speck that is your focus. Instead, imagine before showing off your shot you edit: zoom in to crop out the extraneous imagery and focus just on your star, your main character. Now when you show off the photo, your friends will see that lead singer in full detail. A tighter picture frame allows you to focus on the nuances of this moment. A tighter time frame condenses the imagery to just the essentials, often a single moment, in your character's life. It's also much easier to manage as a writer.

Another aspect to consider when writing short fiction is the concept of *in media res*. The loose translation of this Latin phrase is *in the middle of things*. Short fiction plays the role of interrupting your main character in the middle of a moment. As readers, we get that something happened just before we arrived and, unless you kill off your darling, that something will happen after we leave. We will share a single moment with her. You decide in which moment of her life to introduce us but there will be no long build up to our meeting. This immediacy is gratifying and, often, an expectation when reading short fiction.

CHAPTER 1 EXERCISE

For some of you, your main character's name has been with you for some time. She, herself, has been with you for some time. For others, you may not know how to come up with a name. This can be a fun exercise as it encourages you to consider who and where she will be, and allows you to linger on the significance of the name and what you hope to evoke through it.

My friend, Amy Baldwin, an Arkansan and successful author shares an example of how to brainstorm for a character name below:

> When brainstorming, the names I think of are Winona or Eddie Mae. Something that is Southern because that is what I know and would pull from for a first time attempt to write a short story. I personally would prefer a mixed-gendered name that sounds like a cross between a father's and mother's name — there is something interesting about that. Or a name that requires a long, Southern drawl to pronounce. Claire is too prim, too proper for my character. Mary is too stable, too motherly (although she could be another character). Eddie Mae or Charlie Jane could work — the more cacophonous and unharmonious, perhaps, the better, especially if I think I could explore some inner conflict.

> And what would Winona or Eddie Mae or someone like that be doing in my story?
>
> Birthing a baby?
> Picking cotton?
> Making a cake?
> Handling the death of someone?
> Kissing someone for the first time?
> Having a dream of being someone someday?
>
> Where would they be? That would be easy for me, as I am thinking of the Deep South, mid-to-late summer, hot, humid, thunderstorms, bugs, sweat, the small window unit trying hard to blow cool air into a small house.
>
> But what if I sent her up North? Or to another country or to another time?*

If you're unsure of your main character's name, consider similar aspects as Amy does.

- Is your main character of a certain region, e.g., The Deep South of the United States? Would her name reflect this?
- Is she decidedly female or male or nonbinary? How could her name reflect this?
- Is she a measured, controlled person or does she give way to flights of fancy, or something in between?
- Is she likable and easy to get along with or more reserved, perhaps even prickly?
- What is her central conflict? What will she be doing in the story and discovering about herself? How might her name reflect this?

You may not know how to answer these final questions, and that's okay. Your character will reveal herself to you as you tell her story. We'll spend

---

*From the works of Amy Baldwin.

much more time on this in the Character Development chapter. It's even okay for you to use a placeholder name until something better comes to you and the placeholder may become her name. You'll know it when you find it.

Once you have a name, get a sense of who this person is. Is her name a good fit or is it ill-suited, even ironic? What are some of her dominant and more subtle traits? Will her name suggest something about her character? Follow the paradigm above, created to develop Winona/Eddie Mae, and create your own character. Remember, this is just brainstorming so there are no wrong answers.

CHAPTER 2

Active Language

*The difference between the right word
and the wrong word is the difference between
the lightning and the lightning bug.*

~ Mark Twain

The two best ways to improve your writing are to read the works of good writers and to lose your dependence on weak verbs that create the passive voice. As stated earlier, the reader wants to feel a part of the story and this often proves difficult for the novice writer who depends on passive language. Is, Am, Are, Was, Were, Be, Been Being: the use of these words directly correlates with prescriptive writing, telling your readers what happens rather than pulling them onto the scene and letting them experience it for themselves. To really capture your readers, use precision of language — the exact right word.

Magic happens when you switch from passive to active voice. This proves true for every type of writing: expository, prose, poetry, you name it. But in fiction it transcends into the sublime. In fiction it is the difference between your readers sitting in a chair and hearing about your heroine's escape from a charging gator and your readers running right alongside of her — panting, sweat beading, adrenalin coursing.

Again, this stems from the fact that to-be verbs yield a prescriptive voice. You can feel sure that anytime you use one of the eight to-be verbs, your writing tells more than it shows because the prescriptive voice, like a doctor's prescription, tells you what to do. This may serve as a helpful reminder. Prescriptive voice tells. Active voice describes. Active language allows the writer to show rather than tell. Eliminating those persnickety to-be verbs forces you to think about your active verb choice, which forces you to consider exactly what's going on with your character. To convey this, you must choose the exact right verb. Trust me, when you do it won't be passive.

A form of writing exists that practices the complete elimination of these to-be verbs. English-Prime advocates avoid to-be verbs to communicate and ensure their clarity of meaning. Like most skills, it becomes easier with practice. As a novice writer, this may cause some frustration but you need to start here. Don't get me wrong; I'm not advocating for the use of E-Prime. There is a place for to-be verbs in our language but, in the beginning, to create a world where your reader feels wholly present, you must develop the habit of being precise in your language. Consciously ridding your writing of these verbs will help with this training.

To learn this skill, write as you would normally write. Get your story out of you, no self-edits, no critiques. As much as possible, quiet the critical chatter in your head and just write. Once you feel you have the story out, go back through and begin your edits. Use the Function or Command F keystroke to search for the eight to-be verbs and consider each one. Then replace each one with the precise action word that shows your readers what you see in your mind's eye as your characters' actions. We'll discuss this more in the Editing chapter.

Finally a thought on verb tense. We have discussed active verbs with no specification for whether you choose past or present tense. This is your choice and it should also be an intentional one. I encourage you to choose present tense. This tense tends to create a more vivid and powerful narrative. When we're living the character's life in the moment with him, we don't know if all will be well. When a story is written in past tense, we can presume everything turns out okay because we're hearing about the character's experience after the fact of it. Writing in the present tense is discomforting for many. Try it anyway. Because this is short fiction, the reprieve will come soon enough.

CHAPTER 2 EXERCISE

Write a paragraph or two of description. The subject could be your cat sitting in the window, the way the plants on your balcony move in the wind, the sound of traffic passing by, anything at all, really, and it's even better if there's a little movement or action. Write in your natural voice, without editing.

Once you've completed the description, go back through and highlight all passive verbs (is, am, are, was, were, be, been, being) and replace each one with the precise active verb that better describes the action.

Example: "The plant is blowing in the wind." (With apologies to Mr. Dylan.) This becomes, "The leaves sway in the breeze." or "The flower stem arches against the gale." Notice we have a clearer, specific image of and feel for how the plant looks in the edited statements.

CHAPTER 3

Objective Point of View

There is no such thing as the view from nowhere, or from everywhere for that matter. Our point of view biases our observation, consciously and unconsciously.

~ Noam Shpancer

As a beginning fiction writer, avoid the use of first-person point of view, at least for a while. For both the novice, and for many published writers, first-person may encourage too much self-ingratiation. Instead, begin with a third-person objective point of view.

Imagine standing in the corner of a room, privy to everything that goes on but unnoticeable to the people within. For those familiar, imagine joining Harry Potter under his Invisibility Cloak where he experiences all but remains unseen. You're able to see the characters and their behaviors, hear their conversations, feel the rumble of a passing train, smell and taste the exhaust from its engine. You can then relay all of this to your readers without the characters' awareness. This pretty much sums up writing from an objective point of view. Through your eyes, ears, touch, nose, and mouth (AKA your senses), you share with your readers what happens in that room. A common analogy for this is the fly on the wall. If you put yourself on the scene and describe everything you take in, you will draw in your readers and allow them to feel they're right there with you. The shortest distance to this role of observer is through the active voice (see Chapter 2). Your precision of language will create a sensory experience for your readers that provides access to the scene.

With this third-person objective point of view, your narrator is removed, observing and reporting yet also warm and engaging. Notice I listed the five senses above, but did not include any cognition or opinion. This differs from the oft-used third-person omniscient narrator who is above the scene, in the heads of the characters, a presence from the very start creating a voice between the story and the reader and often passing judgment.

For beginning writers, the omni-viewer frequently tells us what characters are thinking but gives us little of the sensory experience. Think of wearing a blindfold, clothespin on your nose, gloves on and with a sock in your mouth. In other words, you have only your ears to listen to this omniscient narrator tell you what happens. Pretty restrictive. It also can result in uninspired writing, especially when you're learning the craft. If you can just tell me what your characters think, why need to build suspense, create a sensory experience or develop nuance in your characters' behavior? You want to do these latter elements to create a connection with your readers, like when we joined in on the race from the charging alligator in Chapter 2.

An exception to this is the use of third-person close or limited point of view. This is where we're inside the mind of a given character but not in a god-like position, rather more of an over-the-shoulder view. It's similar to first-person but this point of view allows the author to create, and the reader to experience, a closeness with more than one character. It's not limited to just the narrator so we have more freedom. The author Michael Chabon has a talent for close omniscience. J. K. Rowling uses it in her Harry Potter series. We spend most of our time with Harry, creating empathy and learning his story, but Rowling moves us to other characters when needed to better flesh out her full story.

For the beginning writer, however, third-person objective point of view is the best place to start as it forces keen attention to detail. A way to practice this point of view is to write an observational piece (something you'll create in Chapter 5) and fictionalize the details using your personal preferences and what you see in your mind's eye. You'll be inspired by the real world, what happens around you, and from this, you'll create your character's world as something smaller and more intimate. Something you know well. And any gaps in your knowledge can be filled in by observation and research.

So how about a first-person narrator? As mentioned earlier, it's best to hold off using this point of view until you have grown comfortable with the objective. Without this limitation, there's a good chance we get

Objective Point of View

trapped inside the head of this narrator, rattling around, often subjected to meanderings and minutiae. Not always, though. Many great first-person narrators keep us in their heads for long periods of time and it fascinates. *The Catcher in the Rye's* Holden Caulfield comes to mind, though note that many of his thoughts are inspired by those people and things around him; his sensory perception. Since we're at the beginning of this process, you must learn the rules before you can break them. It's better to start off learning the hard stuff so everything else comes easily.

After you've written some stories in third-person objective, and you feel ready to try your hand at first-person, consider how to synchronize the objective point of view with the first-person narrator. To maintain the connection with the reader, it is important to strike a balance between the narrator's insight and his environment. I've referenced Elizabeth Tallent's brilliant short story, *No One's a Mystery,* in Appendix A. Consider how well the narrator keeps us grounded in the setting — not only the truck, but the Wyoming ranchlands. She also maintains complete objectivity. She shares her bias by what she notices and shares with us. But she never takes us into her thoughts, an unusual tactic that helps play into the mystery of the open ending.

Typically, when writing in first-person, you'll want to keep us present, on the scene with your narrator and his fellow characters, and viewing this scene through the color of his particular lens. To do this, consider eye-witness testimony. Five different people can observe the exact same act yet describe five different scenarios. Why? Because each is retelling the act through his or her particular bias. Your first-person narrator will view the world, and retell it for us, through his own bias

An inherently limited perspective, the first-person narrator can share only what he experiences. Unless he hears or smells it, or sees it through a window or crack in the wall (for example), he can't know what happens in a different location — though he can speculate. Typically, what we also get is the privilege of his thoughts, insights and feelings. This creates a strong connection between this narrator and the readers as we often get to know him better than any other character. A certain vulnerability is required as this narrator must let us in, sharing with us his biased view of his world. Rather than an objective perspective, his will be subjective.

Another thing to consider is that your first-person narrator need not always be your main character. There will be times when he is more of a guide, leading us through the scenes, allowing us to know his biased view of each character, including the main character. A well-known example of this is Nick Carraway in Fitzgerald's *The Great Gatsby*. From the sidelines, Nick observes and casts judgment on the characters. We only know what he personally experiences or is told about, and it's all colored through the bias of Nick's perspective.

As the writer, remember to balance the insights of your narrator with the details of the world around him, developing the sensory experience as described in Chapter 5, lest we go dark in the mind of your narrator.

Once you feel ready to consider either point of view, it's possible you'll find yourself unsure of which to choose. In this case, take one scene, a scene you see clearly in your mind's eye or perhaps your introduction to the main character, and write it out both from a third-person objective point of view and from your potential narrator's point of view. Be sure this goes well beyond a pronoun shift and represents the bias of the first-person point of view in one draft and the objectivity of third in the other.

Ultimately, ask yourself and your main character which is the more genuine way of telling his story. Does he want a broad perspective, does he want someone close to him to tell it or does he need to tell it himself? If this seems impossible, asking a question of a fictional person you've only just created, hold off until we get to the Character Development chapter. The essential key in choosing your narrator is to do so mindfully and with intention. It's not a coin toss — someone will always be the better choice to tell this particular character's story in this particular moment of his life.

CHAPTER 3 EXERCISE

This chapter begins by encouraging you to write in the third-person objective point of view. Later, it offers suggestions for shifting to first-person. It's important to first feel confident in the third-person objective point of view.

Take the paragraph or two that you wrote for the Chapter 2 exercise and flesh it out some. In a new paragraph, write in a character — it could be someone in your home or someone you see on the street outside or someone of your imagination. It could even be the cat in the window. Once you've added on another paragraph (free of passive verbs), go back over the work and make sure that the entire passage is objective. There should be no musings, no suppositions, no insight, unless these can be heard by the other characters and, thus, the reader. Removing the passive verbs will likely force this outcome.

Later, once you've finished learning about all 10 guidelines, you can come back to this and repurpose this passage in the first-person. You'll want to incorporate the narrator's insights while still keeping us present on the scene through vivid sensory detail. This balance is important to create the connection with your protagonist and his journey.

Once you've written a passage of narrative in both first and third-person point of view, and given careful consideration to which feels the more genuine choice for your character's story, read both aloud to your friends, your writer's workshop, your family — folks you trust — and ask which feels more authentic, more engaging.

CHAPTER 4

Few Adverbs

The road to hell is paved with adverbs.

~ STEPHEN KING

The explanation in the Preface pretty much sums up this one. If you're precise in your verb use you will have no need for a defining adverb. You'll want to use them, though. They're soothing, as they seem to assure the clarity of our ideas. They're also unnecessary and usually muddle your imagery with redundancy. You needn't tell us that your character *stomped loudly*. The verb *stomp* inherently evokes the notion of loud as one cannot stomp softly or quietly. Perhaps you've written *walked loudly*. This is when you must imagine how the character walks. Picture him in your mind's eye and then show him to us. If he's stomping, this single active verb is enough. No need to say someone *hobbled slowly*, as hobbled means slow-footed. Choosing the precise verb (as discussed in Chapter 2), such as *stomp* or *hobble*, eliminates the need for the defining adverb, helping you to write with more precision and concision.

The focus here is on one-word adverbials as exemplified in the chart in this chapter's exercise. There will be times when it's appropriate to use adverbial phrases and clauses, such as prepositional phrases and phrases of time (e.g. at, in, on); place (e.g. in, on, at, above, beside, below); and manner (e.g. on, by, with, like).

Often, the use of adverbs correlates with our trust in our readers. You may read that and think, *If I don't know my readers, how can I mistrust them?* You can mistrust that they get what you mean and, as writers, we so want our readers to get our meaning. However, if you're clear and precise in your language, your readers will understand. You needn't spell it out for your readers or over explain. You want to write simply because

The Elements of Short Fiction

Because we take in our world through our senses, to ensure your readers connect with your characters you must create a sensory experience within your narrative. To learn this technique, spend some time focusing through your mind's eye. What do you see when you look at your main character? How about her surroundings, her friends, her lifestyle? Pay attention to the sensory details when you're looking through this lens. Imagine you're sitting next to her in the passenger seat of a convertible, driving down a dirt road in Nebraska. See the wind blowing through the corn fields, smell the sulfur of the sprinkler systems in the midday heat, hear their low hum and rhythmic swish and shuffle. Alternatively, inhale the aroma of coffee and hear the buzz of patrons chatting in corners while sunk into deep couches at the local café. Now transcribe this for your readers. Presto — we're on the scene that you've envisioned.

A good way to practice this is to literally record the activity of someone doing something. For example, you could sit in a coffee shop and watch the barista. Notice what she wears, the way she moves and interacts with the customers. Does she make eye contact? Pick at her cuticles? Is she quick to smile? Does she slouch? Attend to how she makes the coffee — is she precise? Messy? What's the environment, otherwise known as your setting? How would you describe the smell? Is it the expected scent of ground coffee or is there an underlying smell of cleaner or, perhaps, the sickly sweet perfume of the patron next to you? Pay attention to each sensory detail while you sit in this café. Take notes. Then write a description of exactly your experience, no fictionalizing just facts and details.

Not a coffee drinker? How about observing your roommate/partner/ parent making dinner or washing the dishes or mowing the lawn? There is no incorrect subject for this type of training, though it's best if your subject remains unaware of your project to maintain their authenticity. The purpose of this practice is to force you to pay attention to each sensory detail during a given experience, like when under the Invisibility Cloak in Chapter 3, and record how these details interact with each other and with the person you've chosen to watch (your main character).

This observation exercise is detailed at the end of this chapter and is the path to third-person objective point of view. It is also something you can practice over and over. Once you understand how to recreate an actual experience, practice transferring the same writing skills — the same attention to detail — to your fiction, describing what you see in your mind's eye. This chapter's exercise is a good way to get started if you're

CHAPTER 5

Five Senses

Don't say the old lady screamed.
Bring her on and let her scream.

~ MARK TWAIN

With each chapter it becomes clearer that these elements work together and do not stand alone. We've already touched on the five senses, developed with the use of active verbs as explained in Chapter 2. Active verbs are what allow your readers to experience the world you're creating and to connect with your characters. As a writer, building a connection between your readers and your characters is your raison d'être, your reason for being. When writing fiction, your goal is to get your readers to feel like they're somewhere else for the time they're with your characters, to think about your characters after they've finished reading their story, and to relate to both.

Even if you don't have publishing as your goal, consider your audience when writing, as this will provide structure for your imagery. Considering the audience is already something you do when writing. When you draft an email or type up a text on your phone, you are no doubt thinking about the person who will receive it. Indeed, if you accidentally text your boss instead of your best friend or spouse, it may leave you feeling awkward. Writing fiction also requires you to consider your audience as this will help guide the mood and tone of your work. If your audience is elementary-aged children, your tone will differ than if it's an adult mystery.

This is not to suggest you worry about your readers' opinions or that you should write for anyone's approval other than your own and the authenticity of your characters. Rather you want to ensure your readers feel present with your characters, so you'll want to consider their viewpoint.

The Elements of Short Fiction

Now rewrite each verb/adverb phrase to be as specific as possible. In the example above, I've simply removed the words *loudly* and *slowly* as *stomped* and *hobbled* suffice. In another example, you might rewrite for the more precise verb: "Mary spoke softly once she entered the cemetery" becomes "Mary whispered once she entered the cemetery." Notice that *whisper* is a more specific verb. It also has a nice onomatopoeic element to it, conveying sound (see Chapter 5).

Few Adverbs

we readers want our focus pulled by your characters' actions, not by the words used to describe that action.

As readers, we like a little rigor, we like to connect the dots, so make us do a little work. A nice example of this from another medium is the art form of Impressionism, where artists use little dabs of paint and allow the mixing of colors to happen in the brain rather than on the canvas, leading to a certain vibrancy. Stand back from a work of this genre, and you see a beautiful scene. Move up close to it, and you see many colored dots. With enough distance, our brain connects these dots to form the image. We want the same from storytelling, yet relying on adverbs mushes all of the dots together and takes away that bit of fun, the tension of your imagery. Be judicious in your description so we readers can work a little to form the images you're spinning. Trust us and trust yourself. Oh, and drop the adverbs.

CHAPTER 4 EXERCISE

Take the passage you've created in the previous exercises and highlight each adverb. If you're not sure whether something is an adverb, err on the side of caution and assume it is. They don't all end with *ly*, such as *very, anywhere, always, ever*, etc. You can look up each one online to determine its grammatical status.

The following chart provides some examples of common adverbs:

Adverbs of Frequency:	Adverbs of Manner:	Adverbs of Degree:	Conjunctive Adverbs:
Always	Well	Very	Finally
Usually	Loudly	Lots	Anyway
Sometimes	Kindly	Somewhat	Certainly
Often	Quickly	Especially	Lately
Occasionally	Cheerfully	Almost	Moreover

~ 15 ~

not sure where to begin. The barista becomes your main character and you make up the details of her life based on your observation of her. For example, if she picks at her nails, make up the reason why. Pay attention to the cadence of her speech and imagine where she's from. Let these details lead you to develop her as a character.

As for crafting this sensory experience, for most, the visual is the easiest to create in writing. Think of all of those adjectives just waiting to describe how something looks. But to create a full sensory experience that will put our readers on the scene, it must feel real, which means we must develop all five of the senses. The one that can be the most fun to play with is sound as we have a particular type of language ready made for this job. Onomatopoeias are words that sound like their meaning and they provide a great auditory experience. The snake *slithered* into the grass, *hissing* as he passed. The *thud* of her head on the desk silenced the room. He *snapped* on the gloves before moving the body.

Interestingly, and happily, these onomatopoeias may also engender the sense of touch. In the list above, slither, thud and snap all have sound and touch qualities. Notice, too, that three of the four are in active verb form. It's easy to assume adjectives are our best friends when describing but, back to the precision of language, it's the verbs that really draw in your readers. Indeed, the way to create the sensory experience is through active language, just as it was described in Chapter 2. Each active verb will convey one or multiple senses. Even adjectives are often overused in this role, so avoid giving a list of them. We typically take in our senses through action. Like noticing the barista's short, nubby nails in the action of her picking at them or serving a coffee. Inhaling the scent of freshly mowed grass in the action of it being trimmed. Seeing the patterned wallpaper as the character passes her hand over it. When you consider these senses, allow your character's experience to wash over you then do your best to record it — just as you did in the coffee shop or your mother's kitchen.

CHAPTER 5 EXERCISE*

The following exercise combines the guidelines from the first five chapters of the book. This process of building on each element will teach you how to approach writing fiction, breaking down the structure into

*Borrowed from the works of Esteban A. Martinez

its individual parts. There is no right or wrong subject matter though it helps to choose something with which you feel familiar. Once you feel comfortable with this type of observational writing, try creating a few pages of fictional narrative, using the five elements as described thus far. This may be inspired by one of your observations or something you've imagined.

1. Select a specific time and place, your setting, and make us see, hear, touch, taste, smell and feel the place you've selected.

2. Select a specific individual. Make sure we know this person's name. Make sure this person actually exists. Show this person engaged in some activity in the time and place you selected. For example, you might describe the barista at your favorite coffee shop, your father in the kitchen washing dishes, your sister mowing the lawn. The possibilities have no end.

   Try to make your reader feel the mood of the scene you've chosen. Also, note that you may begin crafting this piece with first the time and place or first the individual. The order in which to include these elements is up to you. Just remember that you must include all of these elements.

3. You must not break the following rules:

   a. You may not use "to be" verbs (am, are, is, was, were, be, been, being).

   b. You may not use any adverbs ending in *ly* and use as few abstract words as possible (e.g., love, freedom, etc.)

   c. You must write from a third-person objective perspective. Do not write in third-person omniscient or in first-person point of view.

4. Write three to four paragraphs that describe this person, her setting, and her actions so that we experience her, too.

CHAPTER 6
====

Suspense

To create suspense, what you do is withhold information. You don't need a crime or a violent death in the lead to hook your reader.
~ Ted Kooser and Steve Cox

Ah, suspense… the rigor of good fiction and often misunderstood by beginning writers. It's common for new writers to interpret suspense as it appears in action adventure movies. Many early drafts that focus on this element contain car chases, shootings, horrific imagery — but this is often overkill (and usually overdone). Suspense is far subtler than this. It comes from the hint, the mere suggestion that something will happen to the character that we won't want to miss. This hint serves the same purpose in fiction as a thesis statement does in expository writing. It lets us know what we might expect from the reading and then comes back around from time to time to keep us invested in the outcome. "It is the important idea hinted at in the beginning but reserved for the end that creates suspense. Suspense is that unsuspected quality that makes writing vivid, powerful, and nervous, instead of weak and dull" (Martinez).

Watch that you don't confuse suspense with surprise. Instead, think of suspense as surprise's opposite, and as a more effective tool in writing. Surprise lasts a moment, only briefly holding the reader's attention before becoming a memory. Whereas, suspense may hold the reader's attention throughout the hours required for reading a novel.

The hint may be either an open statement or a vague suggestion that something important will happen. Or it may be a situation that, in its very nature, is certain to result in an important outcome, such as a teenager getting ready for his first date. Once you give the hint, you make your readers wait by withholding information. Readers wait for what's coming and the suspense builds through this anticipation. The characters will be actively living their lives during this wait period — and may or may not be waiting themselves. If your main character is in a hospital lounge, awaiting test results, she's waiting right along with us. But in a different circumstance, she may not be waiting in such a deliberate way — in fact, she may not wait at all. However, your readers will wait until you reach the climax and, even here, tension sustains through to the falling action, the story's resolution.

Don't mistake this wait period for just biding the readers' time. The wait period is the heart of the story for it is when we learn about our characters — in particular, our main character. This is another example of how these guidelines work in concert and not linearly, as we're now merging suspense with character development.

So, imagine we meet our main character in class, just as he's glanced over his shoulder to see the girl sitting in the back corner of the room. When he turns back to face us, he is flushed with a trace of a smile. This is all the hint we need to wonder about his relationship with this girl. Show him doing this and we're engaged, curious about what comes next.

As we continue to spend time with him, you'll provide increasingly more information about him. We may learn that he's working up the courage to approach her but is too shy to make the grand gesture of walking to the back of the room. We also learn that he feels conspicuous hanging out in the front until she walks past him. How he negotiates this conflict (approaching her) and his ability to achieve his quest (having a conversation with her) is the heart of this storyline as it's where we learn about who he is as a person. It's also the wait period for us.

As a writer, you make us wait to find out if he summons the courage and whether she returns his interest. Maybe he can't get to her after class — a friend interrupts or the teacher calls — so he must wait until tomorrow. Maybe he asks, but she doesn't immediately accept or decline his invitation. The wait period for the main character is fraught with obstructions and conflict that he must overcome or fail to overcome. How he handles these obstructions reveals himself to us. Quest and conflict are inherent in character development (Chapter 8) because they're inherent in life. We constantly seek and struggle to achieve, celebrating even small victories. The wait period for us is where the tension builds between the characters and the action rises until the climax occurs and we're fulfilled, having learned something about our characters and ourselves in the process.

Don't forget to fulfill the hint, because you don't want to leave us hanging. This is not to say you can't offer an open-ended story for this is not the same as fulfilling the hint. Open endings suggest another scene that will happen right as the characters sort out this one. Fulfilling the hint resolves whatever subtle intrigue you've posed at the beginning to engage our interest. So let us in on the outcome — does he make a move? If so, does she like him, too? Tie up the loose end created by the hint. In other words, fulfill it.

Most stories have more than one suspense arc, meaning there's more than one cycle of hint > wait > fulfillment. Short stories tend not to have more than a couple; however in a novel you can have one overarching element of suspense (will good win out over evil) and then many smaller cycles or suspense arcs under the umbrella of this grand one. The twists and turns of your character's journey will determine the way suspense shows up in your story.

While the hint doesn't have to come in the opening line, it usually will in short fiction. Take a look at the collection of opening lines listed below. Two begin a novel (one 288 pages long; one 422). Two begin a short story (one flash fiction; one a traditional short story). Two give a more obvious hint in the first line, two are more subtle.

> "Many years later, as he faced the firing squad, Colonel Aureliano Buendia was to remember that distant afternoon when his father took him to discover ice." ~ Gabriel Garcia Marquez *100 Years of Solitude*
>
> This is the start of a long novel and includes the hint. This hint comes from the stark contrast between something shocking and presumably criminal (facing a firing squad) and something simplistic and innocent (the memory of discovering ice with his father). We are curious about why he's in his current predicament, especially when it seems he had a normal childhood with a loving father. The opening phrase, *Many years later*, lets us know that we'll be rewarded for our curiosity because Marquez indicates we'll cover some breadth of Buendia's life.

"Knowing that Mrs. Mallard was afflicted with a heart trouble, great care was taken to break to her as gently as possible the news of her husband's death." ~ Kate Chopin *The Story of an Hour*

The opening line of this flash fiction short story introduces us to our main character, Mrs. Mallard, and gives us two significant pieces of suggestive info — she has heart trouble and she's about to learn of her husband's death. We've arrived just in time!

"Besides the neutral expression that she wore when she was alone, Mrs. Freeman had two others, forward and reverse, that she used for all her human dealings." ~ Flannery O'Connor *Good Country People*

O'Connor's first line introduces us to one of the characters of this short story and the hint is subtle, something you recognize more clearly on a second reading. Notice that it does create some intrigue about Mrs. Freeman. We wonder about her peculiar expressions, "forward and reverse," and what we're to discover about her "human dealings." Upon reading the story, we discover that this final phrasing foreshadows the theme of the story. It is quite deft writing on the part of O'Connor.

> "If you really want to hear about it, the first thing you'll probably want to know is where I was born, and what my lousy childhood was like, and how my parents were occupied and all before they had me..." ~ J.D. Salinger *Catcher in the Rye*

What Salinger so uniquely hints at is not only the story of Holden's life, but also of Holden's personality, his character. His voice is so distinctive, anyone familiar with the book can recognize it even out of context. And this distinction intrigues us, as does such a frank description of his childhood. We're curious where he is now so want to stick around to find out. And this is the purpose of all hints, to keep the reader engaged. Note that the point of view here uses first-person and eliminates the fourth wall by having Holden speak directly to us. It shows Salinger's mastery of the craft.

CHAPTER 6 EXERCISE*

To introduce a hint and create a feeling of suspense, the most important word or idea in a sentence, a paragraph, or a story should typically come at the end, especially for beginning writers. This is called the End Position and it is essential in creating suspense. Notice that Marquez's and Chopin's opening lines use the end position technique.

Write 10 different sentences that use this idea of the end position. This means you will save your most vigorous and telling details for the end of the sentence.

Then, choose one of these 10 sentences, perhaps the one that fired off an idea of the character when you wrote it, and create a two-page piece of fiction that begins with this sentence. Develop the structure of suspense over the course of the narrative, making us learn about the character while we wait for the concluding fulfillment. Be sure to include all of the elements described in Chapters 1 through 5.

Borrowed from the works of Esteban A. Martinez

CHAPTER 7

Emotion

I try to tell a story the way someone would tell you a story in a bar, with the same kind of timing and pacing.
~ CHUCK PALAHNIUK

Have you ever watched a scary movie with the sound off? How about watching an onscreen car chase in silence? Consider how differently these scenes affect the audience with and without sound. Without the low thumps of the bass line and the escalating rumble of the timpani drums, our heart rate remains steady, our breathing calm. Turn up the volume and we're on the edge of our seats. We can be completely manipulated — and even know it — and still give in to the orchestrations of the film.

Storytellers need to create a similar emotional tug for our readers and, in the absence of sound, we do this through pacing, a tool that controls the speed or rhythm of your story. The goal is to manipulate your readers' emotions, a word that has developed a bad rap over the years. We hear it and often think of con artists or relationships with lots of drama. For fiction, think of it in a purer sense. To manipulate means to change the shape of something.

Through managing your pacing, you change the shape of your readers' emotions; one of your principal goals as a writer.

Much of what we've discussed so far addresses how you show us your character. You put your readers on the scene so we can experience what your character does and get to know him. So, now that you've shown me his tears you must make me believe that he's sad. Alternatively, make me believe he's faking it to dupe another character. Make the scene *feel* real so the readers will believe what their senses show them. The beauty of fiction is that your characters can be whoever you want — as long as your readers believe it. The pacing you use is how you get our buy in. In other words, seeing is not enough to believe in writing.

First, you show me, next you manipulate me with the pacing so I feel the characters' emotions, and then I believe what I see. Just like with music in a movie. If you turn down the sound at the scary parts, I don't feel scared. If the pacing does not support the character's actions, I won't feel how he's feeling. Also like music in films, the reader is usually unaware of this type of manipulation. We don't want to stop and think about how the pacing is making us feel, we just want to feel it. Even though we know we're reading fiction, we still want the suspension of disbelief.

To accomplish this, your pacing must match your content. It should put us on the edge of our seats or have us reclined in repose, depending on the circumstance. We want to feel the same emotions the characters feel. When they're scared, we want to feel scared. When they're feeling calm, we want this. If they feel uneasy, we want to feel this, too. Without proper pacing, we cannot connect to the characters' emotions and we become observers rather than participants.

So, if your character is excited or nervous because he's working up the courage to approach the girl of his dreams, your pacing should be rough, staccato, breathless. This does not mean that your sentences will be, though they can. It's your phrasing that will shorten, so you could have a long sentence with short phrases. If you want me to believe that your character is calm, governing his emotions as best as possible, your phrasing will be long and languid.

As has already been stated, these elements work in concert. Here is another example of this, for the passive voice is indirect and indirect writing is weak, preventing the readers' emotional buy in. You want your writing to have emotional vigor and this comes from a direct, active voice. Besides eliminating passive verbs (see Chapter 2), you should also state your ideas as directly as possible. Avoid halfway statements and apologies, often indicated by words like "seemed to be" and "looked as if." So rather than write, 'It seems as if the river has breached the dam' write 'The river has breached the dam.'

Once you hone the skill of manipulating readers through pacing, you can play with this. For example, perhaps your readers know that your character is nervous but the other characters think he's calm. Your pacing and sensory description (what you show us) will reflect his manipulation of the characters but not of us, the readers.

CHAPTER 7 EXERCISE

Take the narrative piece you've been developing and highlight the scenes that should evoke an emotional response in your readers. This needn't be some big emotion, it could be something small that piques our curiosity, or tugs at our heart strings. It could cause us a little worry, or put a smile on our faces.

Once you've highlighted these scenes, take a look at the way you've presented the language. Does the phrasing support the emotion you want us to feel? If you want us to feel worry or intrigue, is the phasing short and breathless? If you want us to feel at ease, is the phrasing languid? Consider the story of Joaquin in the cucumber field from Appendix A. Let's look at a couple of the sentences from there:

> "Joaquin pats the pockets of his faded denim cover-alls causing small exhalations of dust. The red-dirt fingers of his left hand stop at his right breast pocket. His hands look as though they belong to an old man, wrinkled and hard, but his face shows only sixteen, maybe eighteen years."

These opening statements set the stage for this flash fiction. They introduce us to the character and do so in a way that we feel present on the scene — we can see, hear and feel Joaquin's movements. We don't feel any worry or alarm. We're content just to be introduced as he seems content and unhurried. Notice the phrasing of each sentence is long and controlled.

Now consider the final statements:

> "Joaquin's hands shoot into and disappear in the cucumber patch. They reappear, each hand gripping several cucumbers, each hand gliding toward the bucket. He releases the cucumbers. They hit the bottom of the bucket and thud. His hands shoot into the patch again, glide to the bucket, release the fruit."

The sentences here are about the same length as the first set, but the phrasing is short. The breaks in imagery, set off by the commas, make us rush through the reading, starting and stopping, creating a breathless feeling. And not only does the pacing cause this breathless feeling but also the imagery and use of repetitive phrases such as *hands shoot* and *each hand*. Words like *gripping* and *thud* help us to see and hear Joaquin (keeping us present) and the words' connotation (the emotion they evoke) is foreboding.

Rework the statements you've highlighted in your narrative to ensure the pacing matches the emotion you wish to evoke from your readers.

CHAPTER 8

Character Development

> *When characters are really alive before their author the latter does nothing but follow them in their action.*
> ~ Luigi Pirandello

It probably seems Character Development should come earlier in the list. I keep pressing the point of character-driven fiction and creating a connection between the reader and your main character. But, remember, the elements don't work linearly. You'll layer them, allowing one to create the next and reflect on the previous.

If your main character is interesting — and all characters are interesting if they're honest, vulnerable and real — then the story just shows up. Have you ever heard someone describe a singer's talent by saying, "She could sing the phone book and I'd love it"? Character development is similar. If your character is compelling, what she does is less important. She could be singing the phone book, or even the entries on a spreadsheet, and we'd enjoy it if we find her real, believable, and we understand something about ourselves through her.

So, if someone were to ask, "What's your story about?" you should rework that in your mind to "Who is your story about?" Everything that happens in your narrative must, in some way, further the development of your main character. Don't focus on the what, focus on the who. Put yourself in your character's shoes. Walk around. Ask her what she wants, why her story needs to be told. Determine the shape of the story by exploring which piece of her life she needs to share.

Creating a compelling character requires that she lay herself open to the readers, really show us who she is, and become vulnerable before us —

which, naturally, requires this of you. One of the most challenging aspects of writing any kind of narrative, whether fiction or nonfiction, is the vulnerability required of the author. You will write about what you are thinking and feeling at the time of the experience being shared. It can be tough. It requires mining your own feelings, lowering your armor and being honest with the truth of your story. While this can feel hard, it's the only way to create a believable character. And creating a believable character is how we readers will connect to her and, again, this connection is your goal as a writer.

CHANGE

To state the rather obvious, character development requires that your character develop in some way. There must be a change in her perspective, her relationship with another character, how she views herself and/or her world. Indeed, to achieve a work of literary merit, your reader will gain a greater understanding of the main character and, thus, himself through this change in your protagonist. By the end of the story, the reader discovers something that he hadn't before, something that is often unexpected.

Time, and its passing, is a fundamental element of all narratives, written or lived. A genuine narrative does not merely describe a static situation, it shows what has occurred over time. As we know from our own lives, time is measured by change. Consider a relative you meet when she's two years old, maybe a niece, and then see again after five years. Five years isn't so long for you but that girl has gone from a toddler, barely able to speak, to a young person with ideas and passions of her own. In other words, a lot of change has occurred for her in those five years.

Imagine running into your best bud from middle school. The first thing he says when he sees you? "You haven't changed a bit!" You smile and accept his intended compliment but think to yourself, *I am completely different.* You know you may basically look the same but you have evolved since middle school into a different, more dynamic person. Both of these scenarios represent change occurring over time.

As mentioned earlier, in short fiction, even though your narrative will not cover the span of five or ten years, your character will still demonstrate a shift over the short duration of your story. This shift, and how your character responds to it, is the reason for the story, as it's how we learn about both the character and ourselves.

In general, this change will come through an evolution of sorts but there are successful main characters who devolve over the time spent with the readers. If you develop an authentic character, you'll know which it will be for her. You'll know whether she changes through growth and taking steps forward in her life or changes through taking steps backward, losing her way in the process.

Following are the various kinds of change in any narrative — via Esteban Martinez:

1. A change in the relationship of characters to one another;
2. A change in the relation between a character and his environment;
3. A change within the character himself brought about by his environment or by other characters or by a deep physical or spiritual experience;
4. A change in the reader's knowledge of the character;
5. A change in the knowledge that some characters in the story have about other characters.

You may feel you know your character inside and out. That you understand her motivations, her fears, her aspirations, so the change she undergoes will be obvious. But often, beginning writers aren't sure about this main character and how she'll anchor the story. A helpful tactic to overcome this is to have a conversation with her and have her answer in her own voice. Ask and have her answer the six W questions:

- Who is the story about (who is she)?
- Where is she (setting)?
- What is she doing (actions and behavior)?
- When is she doing this (time frame)?
- Why is she doing this (what motivates her actions)?
- How does she succeed or fail (how does she change)?

Answering these six W questions helps to guarantee a round character who moves through the stages of a complete, well-shaped story no matter if it's 10 pages or 100.

Writing the answers in her voice will help her to come alive and show you how to guide her story. Does she greet people in short, terse phrases with little eye contact — suggesting she's private, shy, reluctant to share too much? Does she talk easily with everyone, including strangers — conveying a bold, outgoing personality? When faced with conflict, does she leap to resolve it or does she need time to sort through the various scenarios and possible solutions? How your characters speak will match their personalities, unless they're intentionally deceiving another character. We should know, though. Figure out who your main character is based on how she changes and speaks with other characters. The W questions will help you to discover both.

OBSTRUCTED NARRATIVE

Once you have a feel for who she is and which moment in her life she's sharing with us, you can start to throw some obstacles in her way. As fiction writers, we must learn to embrace the concept of an obstructed narrative. Sure, the change in your narrative may occur without interruption from any source, but this is not how life goes (nor would it make for much of an interesting story). How happy are you if, on your regular route to work/the grocery store/to pick up your kids, you make every single traffic light? This isn't the greatest of achievements and yet you notice and may even celebrate. Why? Because you've just had a moment without stop lights interrupting your drive, and there are usually interruptions in the course of a day.

Your narrative should adhere to this same principle. Remember the guy who's trying to build up the courage to ask out the girl in the back of the classroom (from the Suspense chapter)? If he just gets up, walks to the back of the room, asks her out, she says yes, and they make their way to the café, we may feel happy for them both but we haven't learned anything about them. No information has been shared. Make the story interesting by throwing in all sorts of obstacles and let your character struggle to overcome them. Watching how he deals with these challenges will reveal his character to us and help us to better relate to him. Ultimately, your main character is on a quest for something (a date with a girl) and we learn about his fears, desires, hopes and dreams through how he deals with the conflict of achieving this quest. Quest and conflict are rooted in life — we are regularly seeking something, and often we run into some trouble in obtaining it. Thus, this construct of quest and conflict is also rooted in good fiction.

INDIRECT CHARACTERIZATION

As mentioned, you'll need to show us the many aspects of your character for us to form a true connection. And this showing must happen gradually, the peeling of an onion, as it were. This creates an indirect characterization that combines the concepts of change and obstructed narrative. To illustrate this point, let's do a little guided imagery. To borrow from our example in Chapter 6, I want you to imagine you're on a first date (and please don't let your current relationship status hamper this little journey — it's fiction!).

So, imagine you're on a first date with someone who you find attractive, and you're feeling a little nervous but also excited about the evening. The two of you arrive at the restaurant, are seated at your table and given menus. Just as you start to peruse the dinner choices, your date leans across the table and says, "Just so you know, I am the funniest person I know. I mean, I will have you laughing all night long!" Okay, you think to yourself, that's good, you guess. You like to laugh, right?

Now imagine the same opening scene, followed by a comment your date makes to the server that has you and the server chuckling. Then, you're chatting about how you met and your date says something that makes you smile. By the end of the evening, you realize you've been smiling if not fully laughing for most of it. Now, which date would you prefer? It's an obvious answer, isn't it? Most of us would prefer to be on the date where we're so in the moment and sharing such a genuine connection that we enjoy it without effort. As opposed to being told our date is funny, all the while waiting to laugh.

This guided imagery teaches the difference between your main character slowly revealing herself and just telling us who she is. The latter is unnatural and stilted. Despite the riddle having a fairly obvious answer, too often beginning writers create characters more like the first scenario; the date who announces the coming humor. One who tells rather than shows. Any hope of a connection is limited to our heads while cutting us off from our hearts.

I use these bodily terms figuratively, of course, but they're important constructs to consider as writers. Yes, you want to appeal to the intellect of your readers and challenge them to see someone or something differently through your writing, but you must also connect to your readers' emotions and their experiences. We want to feel differently — about your characters and, ultimately, ourselves — after spending time with your story. Thus you'll want to employ the sensory description and character development to really show us your protagonist.

What's tricky is you also want to maintain the element of suspense and avoid over-delivering your character, over-describing her. As mentioned earlier, allow readers to connect the dots. Create rigor for us — as mentioned in Chapter 4, our brains like to figure out how things fit together. So while you should show rather than tell, you needn't show everything. If your character enters the room, we can assume it's through the door so you needn't specify this. However, if she enters through the window or, better yet, removes a ceiling panel and drops down to her desk, you need to show this to us as it speaks to her character.

SECONDARY CHARACTERS

Your main character also develops through the relationship between her and your secondary characters. These are the family members, friends, coworkers, random acquaintances, even strangers that make up her world and are the other people in your story. They're of great importance to developing your main character. To help illustrate the relationship between main and supporting characters, imagine something round and spherical versus something flat and two-dimensional. Your main character will be round, full, wholly developed; the secondary characters will be relatively flat. Secondary characters are one of our best vehicles for seeing all sides of the main character. So think of the secondary characters as flat like a mirror, able to reflect the traits of the main character.

Remember in Chapter 1 when we discussed setting and how this is important because people behave differently in different environments? Well, the same can be said for your secondary characters. Your main character will likely behave one way with one of these minor characters, another way with a different minor character, and perhaps a third way when all are together.

As with setting, this does not mean that your main character is pretending or faking (though you may like her to if appropriate for the moment), this just means different people, like different settings, bring out different sides of us. Because of this, you'll want to choose your secondary characters thoughtfully and intentionally. We'll see different facets of your main character in the mirror that is each minor character. Be mindful of how they appear in your story for they will reflect to us your star.

Dialogue is another great tool for allowing us to get to know your characters. Think of the friends who are dear to you yet who you've known only a few years. How have you become so close? Probably from the two of you sharing your stories over a glass of wine, cup of coffee, run in the park or swing on the playground. You'll use the dialogue between your main character and the secondary characters in the same way — to help them learn about each other and, moreover, to allow us to learn about them. Dialogue also provides the auditory experience that helps put your readers in the room with your characters.

Because we're discussing the writing of short fiction, be wary of having too many players. While the secondary characters are relatively flat they are not mere shells of a character. If you have too many in too few pages, each runs the risk of being superficial and, thus, untrustworthy. Whether your readers like your characters or not is unimportant, but we must believe what they show us about the main character so we learn about her journey.

WRITE FOR TRUTH, NOT FOR TRIBUTE

On this note, let's take a moment to address the need for your readers to like your characters. It's natural; we spend all of this time with these fictional beings, we want our readers to like them. But your readers won't always like them and certainly won't always like their actions. This is okay. Avoid writing to please your readers and, instead, write the truth of your characters' stories.

Because your characters must seem real, they must seem human.

> A character seems convincing when the reader has several conflicting emotions about her. A character who is all goodness is not convincing, nor is one whom we merely despise. To convince us, a character must make us admire her and despise her; understand why she does something yet deplore her doing it. Generally, she will be a character whose fundamental traits will make us sympathize with her under certain circumstances and make us condemn her in others. — Martinez

Without this balance, the main character will be flat and unconvincing rather than round and believable.

Earlier, I mentioned appealing to both the head and the heart of your reader. It's okay if your readers don't like your characters and it's okay if they do. What you don't want is for your readers to feel indifferent, disconnected. I remember when I first read *A Prayer for Owen Meany* by John Irving. I despised Owen for the first chunk of the book; I couldn't understand how John, the narrator, spent so much time with him. By the end of the novel, however, I slowed down my reading because I didn't want my relationship with Owen to end, and I cried once it did. Irving stirred in me a passionate, invested connection to his complex titular character. And this experience occurs with many great stories.

This is your goal, too. At the very least you want your readers to sympathize with your main character, to understand why she's doing something even if it's not the choice the readers would make. At best, you want to evoke an empathic response from your readers where they feel right there in your main character's shoes, experiencing every high and low right along with her. So, it's okay if the readers don't like your character; they must only believe in and relate to her in some way. This belief in her behavior allows readers to assess their own choices in the same circumstance, thus learning more about themselves through your characters' stories.

CHAPTER 8 EXERCISE

You can use your ongoing narrative begun at the end of Chapter 5 or do this as a stand-alone exercise.

Get yourself to a public setting — a coffee shop, book store, park bench. It doesn't matter much as long as it's not super loud. You'll want to be able to hear the conversations of passers by. Be sure to have a paper and pen or your notes app open. Now sit and pay attention to the snippets of conversation you hear as people walk past you. You'll no doubt hear statements that catch your ear and your curiosity. The isolated statements from people on the move are preferable to listening in on the conversation of someone sitting next to you. In this exercise, you want to imagine the topic of the person's conversation. If you're privy to the full chat, you need not imagine.

You'll then take one or several of these snippets and develop a character around it. Your character could be the one who says it. The out-of-context statement could inform your character's personality. You could give the line to a secondary character to say to your protagonist. Your goal is to build a scene from your imagination that's born out of this one overheard line.

For example, I remember sitting on the patio of a cafe when two people walked by. I overheard one say to the other, "...and then I had to roll her under the bushes and I could barely see it was so dark." What a statement, right? What could she have been talking about? It may have been innocuous — maybe her dog was stuck and she was trying to help. It may have been more nefarious. I have no idea, but making up a story around this statement is a fun character development exercise and allows my imagination to run wild creating the kind of person who would say this.

Once you start this practice, you'll find you regularly notice enticing snippets of conversation wherever you are. And not only is this a great exercise for character development, it's also a useful tool for overcoming writer's block. If you feel stuck and need some inspiration, go outside and listen to other people's chatter — and observe how they behave. Remember in Chapter 5 (Five Senses) when I asked you to notice if the barista at the coffee shop bites her nails and to consider why? All of these work together to create a single, character-driven narrative.

CHAPTER 9

Distorting the Truth

When I was a kid, they called me a liar. Now that I'm all grown up, they call me a writer.

~ Isaac Singer

This may seem an obvious one, given we're learning to write fiction. However for many beginning writers, it's difficult to separate themselves from their own stories, from the people in their lives, and from remembering and transcribing the exact details.

One problem with sticking too close to the story is that the focus shifts away from the character. We don't care if you get all of the details right — this isn't a memoir or nonfiction — what we care about is whether she found the courage and took the risk to move out of that small town to pursue a college degree. Sticking too closely to the story also locks you in as a writer. Remember, in fiction, your characters can do whatever you want and be whomever you want, we readers just have to believe it (see Character Development). Embrace this freedom and manipulate the details to distort the truth.

Because you are your greatest resource, you will draw from your life but in more of an amalgamation. You'll take your favorite trait of your mom's, the quirkiest trait of your brother, the most laudable trait in your dad, the most irritating trait in your aunt and put them into one character. This way you have bits and pieces that you love, or at least that you know, and a humanly complex character, but you're not wedded to the truth of any one real person's story.

This is yet another example of how these elements work in concert. At the end of Chapter 5, you're asked to observe someone doing something to teach the recreation of each nuance, every detail of the character and her environment so that your readers feel present in your writing. So, we've almost come full circle. That early exercise of sitting in a coffee shop and recording every detail to recreate the scene has returned.

The more you write, the more you should notice interesting details that show up in your everyday activities. Notice how the cashier at the grocery store interacts with you. Notice how the guy walking his dog down your sidewalk responds to his pet. Notice how the cab driver tilts his head while straining to hear you. Notice, notice, notice. These details will begin to jump out at you and when they are particularly intriguing, write them down on a handy scrap of paper in your pocket or the notes app of your phone. Do this so that you may give these details to your future characters. Since you don't know any of these people, the story you make up around these notable details must be fiction. And don't only notice but imagine what it's like to inhabit those lives, however temporarily you're observing. Just like you imagined the story around the snippet of conversation you overheard in the Chapter 8 exercise. Noticing and applying these details will enable you to develop the humanity around these personality traits that have intrigued you. This will enable you to develop a fully round, complex and believable character who is born out of your imagination.

Research has an important place in writing fiction to ensure you get the facts right — the symptoms of Huntington's Disease, the date of Lincoln's assassination, the process for obtaining financial aid — but, ultimately, you are your greatest resource, so you must learn to pay attention to your life. And then distort it to create a work of literary merit.

CHAPTER 9 EXERCISE

As suggested in this chapter, think of a few people close to you. Maybe your mom or dad, a sibling, a childhood friend, a colleague. Now make a list of their most unique, funny, irritating, and endearing traits. Make sure you have a few different people and a few different traits. Write them all down.

Now create a fictional character using some of these traits. You might write the traits on slips of paper and segregate them by type (a group of endearments; a group of irritants; etc.) and draw one from each pile to give to your character, making her round and human. Give her a name and allow her name and her traits to create her identity in your mind.

Next, think of a memorable moment. This needn't be a big momentous memory where your life changed — though it could be. It could also be a time when you had a really good cup of coffee and sipped it from the cozy warmth of your home or the coffee shop on a cold, dreary day.

Write a few paragraphs where this new character lives out one of your memories. Be sure it's as she would live it, based on this identity you've created, not how you lived it. In other words, distort the truth of your experience.

CHAPTER 10

Editing

Get it down. Take chances. It may be bad, but it's the only way you can do anything really good.
~ William Faulkner

I believe more in the scissors than I do in the pencil.
~ Truman Capote

It's true that many writers often imagine their work published, maybe showing up on the *New York Times* bestsellers list or even winning a Pulitzer. There's nothing wrong with this, you may even let it inspire you. The problem can come when you consider this final element: Editing. You may ask yourself, *Why must I spend all this time editing my story when I'll be working with a publisher who will do that for me?* Sure, I could remind you how difficult it is to get an unaffiliated, non-represented manuscript into the hands of an acquisitions editor, but this is not why editing is so important to your work.

Only you know your characters inside and out. Only you know what motivates him to leave his career of 20 years to pursue his own start-up. It's not just for the freedom from a desk job or because he hates his boss, it's more deeply rooted than this. Remember from the list of elements in this book's introduction: putting your words on paper (or screen) to create a first draft is the equivalent of putting clay on a wheel. This first draft allows you to begin the work. And it's the only way to a well-crafted completed story. Once you have the lump of clay, you must shape it into something beautiful; shape your words to tell this man's story. Editing and the work of revision is the true rigor of your writing and it's where you watch your characters come alive.

Editing

Editing can be taxing, for sure, so it helps to take breaks. Leave your characters alone for a while and then come back to them with fresh eyes and a fresh perspective. They'll be clearer for it and you'll be better equipped to show the readers this clarity. As mentioned in Chapter 2, while you're in the throes of writing, try as much as possible not to self-edit along the way.

You wear two hats when composing: that of the writer and that of the editor. These two folks are often at odds, so it's best to keep them separated, never in the same room at the same time. If you constantly stop to critique your every sentence, you risk curtailing the creativity of the moment by over-thinking each word or image. Likewise, when you're editing, don't be afraid to cut a brilliant line of dialogue if it's inauthentic for this character in this moment. Save it for another story.

Because your real life is your richest resource, you'll want to rely on the practices you learned in the Chapter 5 exercise. And, as addressed in Chapter 9, you'll also need to fictionalize the details you observe. This will have you imagining why certain behaviors occur and this explanation will speak to your character's reason for being. Consider the barista's nervous tic of picking at her fingernails. Perhaps she was a young child when her parents divorced and during this process they often fought. She was too little to engage or understand and found it stressful so she channeled her anxiety and unspent energy into nail-picking. I made up this explanation in this moment. I imagined what might cause someone to pick at their nails and allowed it to be a character developing point. It could just as easily be from constant hand-washing required for her barista job. What's important here is how you understand your character and her motivations. This will make her feel real.

The earlier suggestion to minimize and repurpose to-be verbs will assist in this. Tap into your mind's eye and be clear on the actions of your character. How do you see her? What, precisely, is she doing? As suggested in Chapter 2, use your application's search function to find all eight to-be verbs then choose the best active verb replacement to let your readers see in their mind's eye what you see in yours. While you're at it, you'll likely find unnecessary adverbs, too. This exercise technically focuses on the details, and ultimately develops a complete character.

When I was in college, I was required to write a thesis for graduation. I found it enjoyable to spend my mornings doing research and my afternoons typing away. I'm a fast typist so composing on the computer allowed my words to keep up with my thinking. Still, I had a great deal of trouble with my introduction. How to launch an engaging argument to sustain a 50-page paper? I met with my Thesis Advisor who recommended I hand-write my introduction. At first, this seemed an odd suggestion but I was willing to try anything. What happened is a useful lesson.

This exercise forced me to slow down and step back from my work. No longer could I type as fast as my thought process. I had to create distance between me and my work, and my entire paper benefited from it. Indeed, there is much research to suggest the benefits of writing in longhand. Doing so increases brain power (K. James, Indiana University); it results in better composition (University of Wisconsin study); it increases mental acuity *(Wall Street Journal);* and it promotes creative flow.

Even if you're not a fast typist, or if you don't compose on the screen, consider physically moving away from the bulk of your work and taking a pad of paper to examine a single scene. Write it out in longhand and read it aloud to yourself. How does it sound? Does it promote the character and her journey as you envision and as she requires? This close inspection of a single moment will enable you to better sort out your storyline.

A difficult exercise for many writers is to pull yourself out of the trees to view the forest of your work. You'll need a way to look at the whole of your narrative. As mentioned, you know your characters and their motivations so well, you may find yourself mesmerized by their actions, in the zone — a sublime place for any activity. How, then, do you shut this off to view the work from a distance? How do you make cuts to their brilliance? You want to move away from only describing her facial gesture or nervous tic to showing the energy around these movements. Show the sum of the parts, if you will, to create these complex, vulnerable humans.

Let's also talk a bit about storyboards and outlines. Because this book teaches the writing of short fiction, this may seem irrelevant for your composition — it's not so much content to manage — but you'll need some means for organizing your thoughts, your characters, and your scenes. A traditional outline can work. I have a friend who uses an Excel spreadsheet, where each column holds a scene or bit of description; so you could try out this strategy. There's no wrong answer regarding your process, just so the end result is organized. You'll be grateful for it when you're on page 25 and you realize the scene you're writing better belongs back on page 10, except what to do with the scene that's currently on page

10? If your scenes are well organized, it will be easier for you to rearrange them if necessary.

A useful tool for a storyboard is to get the 3" x 5" sticky notes and write a single scene on each one. The reason I like sticky notes is twofold. First, you can put them up on the wall and step back, enabling you to see the whole of your narrative at once. This is useful for gauging the arc of the suspense and the shape of the story. Second, it's easy to move scenes around. You could also use a bulletin board, push pins, and actual index cards. One of my authors uses 3" x 5" sticky notes on a piece of foam board so he can carry the storyboard around with him, enabling him to work from his home office, his dining room, or his back patio.

You might also consider using a more traditional outline. To begin this outline, introduce your main character and your main secondary character: give their names and a brief description of each. Next, describe the setting. Recall the often-overlooked importance of place from Chapter 1. Be specific here, know where your story occurs and how this affects the characters. Then, describe the anticipated quest and conflict — what is your character seeking and what obstructions might you put in his way. The key word here is "anticipated," for the development is fluid so this may change as you compose. You'll then describe the anticipated change in your main character. Again, you can only anticipate this because the character's development is fluid. An aspect of character-driven fiction is that the character may change differently from what you expected at the beginning, so be open to this. Finally, answer these questions: Why should your readers care about your main character? What is the point of writing this story? Your answers here will help you get to the theme.

You needn't, necessarily, consider the theme while you're writing, as this often occurs without the writer's awareness. But for sure, good fiction is philosophic. Connecting with your readers is your reason for writing and it's through the human experience that we make this connection. Theme is the main idea or underlying message of your story that comments on our humanity. It observes life, makes some determination about life, helps us to understand life by understanding the characters. Think bravery, good vs. evil, redemption, love, forgiveness, etc. These concepts often sum up the theme in works of literary merit.

Whichever organizational tool you choose, it's important that you use one in your revision process.

Creating an outline will also help you get started with your short story as a pre-writing exercise. It may seem peculiar for me to mention a pre-writing exercise here in the Editing chapter, when your first draft is complete. But remember that your first draft is the lump of clay. A pre-writing exercise can help determine what to keep and what to omit. It's also a useful tool before you begin your first draft.

Once you have an idea of your main character and her journey, outlining the steps she takes and the supporting characters who join her can help to guide how you shape her story. One difference between a pre-writing outline and an organizational one is how many and what type of details you have to include. For example, in the pre-writing outline, you'll want to include under Roman Numeral I, some fleshing out of your characters. After your introduction, ask each character 10-15 questions and have the characters answer. I mentioned asking questions of each character in the Character Development chapter as a good way to hear your character's voice. Doing a set of Q&As for each character in the planning phase of your work helps to ensure that you distinguish between the multiple characters' voices and their motives. You'll find a template for this type of outline in Appendix C.

Now that you've learned all 10 elements, you have the tools for writing a full-blown short story. This story should incorporate characterization, suspense, emotion, dialogue and setting. A good length for your first go is 10-15 pages. The following list offers a summation and study guide for creating a complete short story.*

1. **Feeling:** Feeling in fiction is indispensable. It's indispensable not only because readers demand it, but because it's the life force of fiction. It's the life breath of character, setting, dialogue, plot, theme, action, idea, and style.
2. **Subject:** Fiction must be about something.
    a. Write about a world with which you are familiar. The idea is to write about *a* world, not *the* world. With all of the worlds we inhabit, you will never be at a loss for subject matter. And you needn't know everything about a given world — familiarity is relative, after all. Writers typically conceive of a place that is relatively familiar and then gather more precise details through direct observation, inquiry and reading.

Borrowed from the works of Esteban A. Martinez

b. For your subject matter, choose anything in one of your worlds that has stirred a feeling in you: joy, amusement, grief, pity anger, wonder, delight, bliss, adoration, horror, indignation, hatred, contempt, bewilderment, frustration, disappointment, disillusionment, or anything else.

c. Prefer the unusual to the common place as a subject. Because every character is a unique individual, every situation involving this character is unique, and every incident is unique because it happens at a time that never has been before and never will be again.

d. A subject should be at least two subjects. A story with literary merit exists on two levels. If it is a war story, it will not only recount war adventures, but will also illustrate the writer's feeling or philosophy on war. If it is a love story, it will reveal the intricate nature and odd manifestations of love.

3. **Theme:** This is the essential idea or intellectual concept of which the characters and action are specific illustrations. It is the generalized abstractions covering the concrete instances of the story.

4. **Character:** Fiction should be centered about one character.

5. **Background:** The characters move against the background and the action occurs within it.

6. **Information:** A serious reader of fiction expects to receive information. This is one reason why background is so important. The serious reader may expect fiction to teach him something about history — a new philosophical idea, or some large truth about humanity, or some analysis or criticism of society or some revelation about moral or political theories. At the least, the reader would wish for some increased knowledge about psychology through our characters' actions.

7. **Change:** A fundamental element of all narrative is time. A genuine narrative does not merely reveal or describe a static situation, it tells what has occurred in time. Time is measured by means of change.

8. **Obstructed narrative:** Because life tends to have interruptions, and these provide intrigue and challenge for our characters,

obstructed narrative is essential. The writer makes the story interesting by throwing in all sorts of obstructions and letting the characters struggle to overcome them.

9. **Quest and Conflict:** Set your character on a quest of something and create conflicts in her obtaining it. Conflict may exist on one of three planes:

    a. The action may derive from the conflicting will of two people or groups of people, as when the police try to capture a wanted man and this man tries to avoid capture.

    b. The action may derive from the conflicting will of several people.

    c. The action may derive from the conflicting wills within one person, as when someone is attracted to two people at once, or when someone wants to be honest but is tempted to be dishonest, or wants to be brave but is afraid.

10. **Plot:** A writer creates a plot when she sets a character on a quest. This is often the result of some conflict.

CHAPTER 10 EXERCISE

Once you've finished the first draft of your complete short story, the one that incorporates all nine elements discussed, turn off your computer. Then put on some music and cook a meal. Or go outside for a walk, taking deep breaths of fresh air. Maybe build Legos with your kid, or wrestle with your dog. Find some enjoyable, physical, zen-producing activity and fully indulge. In other words, take your mind off your story.

Then, when you're ready, come back to it. Turn on your computer, maybe put on some instrumental music (classical or jazz works best for me), and read through your story, start to finish. This is the time to read with a critical eye. The time to interrupt the flow of your review and make corrections.

I prefer to copy the text to a new document and retitle it (2.0 or by the date) each time I do a significant edit. This allows me to hold onto anything I decide to cut and can help with the organization of my edits. I use track changes and the comment balloons to make notes to myself as I rework.

Editing

This critical review will likely begin with spelling and punctuation. One of the best hacks for correcting errors in syntax and continuity is to read your paper aloud to yourself. Even if we can't explain a grammatical rule, we usually know if one's been broken when we hear it. This is similar to knowing when a musician hits the wrong note, even if we can't play an instrument. This can feel awkward at first, reading your work outloud to yourself, but it's the best way to find these types of errors. And you can't mumble to yourself, you must project. Because you know what you're trying to say, your brain will correct any errors with a silent reading.

Next, you'll focus on the content of your story:

- First reading: Does the story make sense, hang together? Are your characters believable?
- Second reading: Are all nine elements represented?
- Third reading: Workshop
    - Read your story aloud in front of your peers.
    - Before reading, give them specific instructions for the feedback you seek (you'll know your sticking points).
    - After you've read, ask for general impressions, first, and then their take on your requested critique.
    - Take notes of their thoughts. These will help to shape your revision.
    - See **Appendix B** for full Workshop guidelines

Congratulations on creating a corrected, reviewed story! It's time to write your second draft.

APPENDIX A

Stories that Model the Elements

Cucumber Field

By Esteban Martinez

Joaquin pats the pockets of his faded denim coveralls causing small exhalations of dust. The red-dirt fingers of his left hand stop at his right breast pocket. His hands look as though they belong to an old man, wrinkled and hard, but his face shows only sixteen, maybe eighteen, years. His fingers curl then pull out a pair of yellow latex gloves, the kind some people wear to wash dishes. He snaps them from his pocket then begins snugging them on, first the right then the left. As he does this, dried mud falls from the gloves to the cucumber field.

Joaquin walks back to the truck that delivered him to the field with the other migrant workers. Most of them, like Joaquin, have dark skin, some deep brown, some red copper, some the color of the darkest desert sand. At the truck, Joaquin retrieves a wide-brimmed straw hat, puts it on his head, sniffs the hay-scented air, then walks to a row of cucumbers. The sun begins to rise. Roosters crow. A mist, a few feet above the field, begins to disappear.

> Our main character is introduced.
>
> Visual of his clothing suggests many hours of labor.
>
> "small exhalations of dust" is an example of personification (giving human characteristics to an inanimate object) that helps us to connect with the action. We see and feel this image.

> *Active verbs — "curl" and "snaps" and "snugging" — put us on the scene. Note this story uses no passive verbs
>
> *The reference to dish-washing gloves lets us know Joaquin probably brought them from home rather than their being provided by his employer.
>
> All five senses are represented in these few lines, putting us in the cucumber field with the workers.

Appendix A

> This image gives us information about Joaquin. He's athletic, efficient, familiar with the work. And the imagery allows the author to show rather than tell.

A man, "el patron," throws empty five-gallon buckets to the cucumber pickers. Joaquin catches his bucket by the handle, sets it at his feet, then stoops, holding the bucket with his knees.

"Go fast," el patron," says, "make money. One dollar a bucket."

Joaquin reaches for a cucumber, pulls it from its stem, smothers it with his hand, drops it in his bucket then shakes his head in disgust. It takes too much time and too much sweat to fill a bucket with small cucumbers.

A leather-faced man working the row across from Joaquin curses in Spanish. "Chingada!"

Joaquin looks at the man. "What's wrong?"

"These damn cucumbers are too small. Takes twenty minutes to fill a bucket. Chingada!"

> Dialogue reveals character through what they say and how they say it. It also puts us on the scene as we can hear them, tapping into our auditory sense.

The sun beats Joaquin's hat. He nods his head in agreement. "Aye. Too small. But what can we do?"

El patron shouts his words of encouragement again. "Go fast, make money. One dollar a bucket!"

Joaquin's hands shoot into and disappear in the cucumber patch. They reappear, each hand gripping several cucumbers, each hand gliding toward the bucket. He releases the cucumbers. They hit the bottom of the bucket and thud. His hands shoot into the patch again, glide to the bucket, release the fruit. He does this again and again, faster and faster, until his hands become a blur.

Final imagery accomplishes several things:

1. The imagery keeps us in the field with Joaquin and the other workers as we see, hear and feel what they do.

2. The theme of the story — that migrant workers labor hard for little pay — is shown without being told. Joaquin is resigned to his circumstance, "What can we do?" and instead he chooses to pick so fast that his hands become a blur.

3. The pacing matches the content. He's working hard and we feel his labor.

One of These Days
By Gabriel Garcia Marquez

Another great example of pithy, well-developed short fiction, Gabriel Garcia Marquez's *One of These Days* qualifies as flash fiction, writing that is only a few hundred words. Marquez incorporates the elements of short fiction to give us three characters, put us on the scene, and develop theme.

The opening paragraphs introduce us to our main character, Aurelio Escovar. Marquez paints a picture of Escovar through his appearance, the setting, and the action. Notice we see the room and learn about Escovar through his actions. We know he's methodical, precise, a hard worker, and uses antiquated equipment.

We meet the other two characters when Escovar's son interrupts his work to announce the mayor's arrival. Marquez deftly uses this brief exchange to further develop Escovar's character. He does not wish to help the mayor, does not care if the mayor knows this, and is unfazed by the mayor's threats. Note how the dialogue works to reveal these aspects of Escovar's character without Marquez ever telling us. It also keeps us in the moment as we can hear the exchange, using our auditory sense.

The hint is set up in an intriguing way for this story. The opening paragraph seems rather mundane, watching Escovar start his day. But this ordinary behavior also invites us to wonder why we're here. Then the full hint comes when Escovar yells for his son to tell the mayor that he's not in the office, which the mayor would also be able to hear, showing us a deliberate and overt dismissal of the mayor's pain.

When the mayor arrives, perhaps to kill Escovar, he and we see the mayor's pain in his swollen face. Notice the lovely detail Marquez uses to let us see Escovar's shift in feelings: "He closed the drawer with his fingertips." In other words, he is gentle about it. Had Marquez been less specific, "He closed the drawer," we'd be left to guess in what manner. Letting us see that Escovar uses his fingertips, we understand the calm nature of it. In this scene, Marquez also shows us more of the office and its surroundings, confirming that it is, indeed, a poor office, despite Escovar's work ethic.

In the dialogue between Escovar and the mayor, we learn that the mayor has an abscess so the repair must be done without anesthesia to numb

Appendix A

the pain. This exchange, how they speak, how Escovar continues with his methodical practice, how the mayor watches him, develops both characters while tapping into our senses to keep us on the scene.

The paragraphs where the tooth gets extracted give excellent examples of pacing. The phrasing is quick, tense, breathless. We feel what the mayor feels (especially if you've had similar dental work!). The pacing matches the content. Notice how the statement, "Without rancor, rather with a bitter tenderness, he said: 'Now you will pay for our twenty dead men'" shifts back to a more languid, controlled statement. Escovar is now in control and reveals the possibility that he forwent anesthetic for revenge. An act that speaks to theme. For the actual extraction, the pacing returns to clipped and staccato to match the emotional content. Then, again, the final statement here, where the mayor looks at the tooth, is long and controlled. His tooth is out, the trauma has ended.

The final exchange shows us even more of the setting and furthers the idea of the story. In four lines of dialogue we learn that the mayor doesn't just run the town, he is the town. Marquez tells us none of this, rather reveals it through what he shows us in this narrative.

Is it a perfect example of the 10 elements? No. It's a translation from Spanish and translations vary based on the translator. Is it about as close as one can get? Yep.

You can find this story online by searching for "One of These Days by Gabriel Garcia Marquez."

No One's a Mystery
By Elizabeth Tallent

When reading this story, you'll find that this narrative is written from a first person point of view, and it is completely objective. We spend no time in our narrator's mind, yet we know quite a bit about her. Tallent deftly uses imagery to put us in the truck with the narrator and Jack, and this sensory detail lets us understand their relationship and each other.

In the opening paragraph, we immediately know how old our narrator is (18), that it's her birthday, and that someone named "Jack," who is likely her lover given the intimacy of the gift, is a cheap optimist. It's a five-year diary, and is also "light as a dime" with a lock which "didn't seem to want to work." In the action of her "scratching" at the lock (great sound and touch word!), we learn that Jack is married and that our narrator is a secret. This statement that gives us both the image of a failed birthday gift and his adultery is our hint: "I was sitting beside him scratching at the lock, which didn't want to work, when he thought he saw his wife's Cadillac in the distance, coming toward us."

When he sees his wife's car, he pushes the narrator down onto the floor of his truck to hide her and in this action, we learn that he doesn't want his wife to see her, and the narrator's easy compliance suggests it's not the first time this has happened. While there, she shares her view, introducing Jack's character: the floor is dirty, the ashtray smells of the cigarette butts, his jeans are crisp clean, they're listening to country music, and drinking tequila while driving around. That she doesn't know "why his Levi's always bleached like that" suggests that she doesn't take care of anyone's laundry and that his wife takes care of Jack's.

The casualness of their ensuing dialogue gives away their characters. He's annoyed that his wife drives the speed limit, and "can't think of a single habit in a woman that irritates [him] more than that." As if his adultery is somehow less irritating. Yet, the narrator does not pass this judgment. She just tells us what he says and lets us determine its meaning.

The following paragraph and her continued description of the world-as-she-sees-it further develops both characters. Jack doesn't wave, just lifts two fingers. The wife's horn toots "musically" to suggest an upbeat character. Jack is driving "easily eight miles an hour" in contrast to his wife. This detail shows us his recklessness. The details of his boots convey a ranch hand. And, more importantly, they show us how long their affair has gone on — "the same boots he'd been wearing for the two years I'd known him" — so, since she was 16 years old. Notice how she never tells us any of this. She reveals it through the action of the narrative.

Another thing to note in this scene is the pacing. The opening sentences have long, controlled pacing. Our narrator is content, looking at her birthday gift. It remains controlled when Jack pushes her to the floor, letting us know she's not rattled by this. Then, when Jack speaks, the pacing shifts to clipped, rushed phrasing. It switches back to controlled when he sees our narrator is going to stay on the floor, showing that her behavior is not a source of worry, for him or for us. It then switches again to hurried pacing as they continue talking about Jack's wife. Once the wife's car has passed, and the narrator is studying Jack's boots, the pacing returns to slow and controlled, to show us we can feel calm with them.

Tallent gives us the reason for the title through a reference to a Roseanne Cash song and the implied theme of the story. Because this is not a guide to interpreting literature, we won't spend much time on the symbols. Rather note how the dialogue around this song reveals their character, the nature of their relationship, and the point of the story — all through showing in objective detail what occurs in that pickup truck. And the pacing of the dialogue also matches the content. As our narrator gets more defensive, her pacing shortens.

Even the final lines, when Jack assures our narrator that the breath of her imagined baby, Eliza, would not smell like vanilla but like the narrator's milk, "and it's kind of a bittersweet smell, if you want to know the truth," show us that not only is he married but most likely has children of his own. For a man to know the smell of breastmilk suggests an intimacy with his wife in the rearing of their children. And describing it with such a specific word as bittersweet further speaks to the nature of their affair and his conviction that the narrator will tire of it and him.

You can find this story online by searching for "No One's a Mystery by Elizabeth Tallent."

APPENDIX B

Writing Workshop Guidelines

The writing workshop is an interesting paradox. It is both the best tool for improving writing and often the most dreaded. A storied 1973 study on fears by Bruskin and Associates determined that most respondents selected public speaking more often than any other as their greatest fear, including their own death (Watson 9). I share this statistic with my students. It helps to alleviate their anxiety by letting them know that those who consider dropping the course to avoid the workshop are not alone in their fear of public speaking. I also remind them that everyone in the class must do this, so they're united in solidarity

What adds to the anxiety in a creative writing course is that this public speaking is the reading of a personal writing. Writing creatively already requires great vulnerability. Reading one's work aloud to a group exponentially increases this vulnerability.

Fortunately, I've figured out a technique that solves multiple concerns when conducting a workshop.

The tools required are a screen and a means to project each student's writing upon this screen. A document camera works well, or you can have students submit their work electronically and cast it on the screen from your LMS/inbox. This conserves paper and avoids the problem of students forgetting to bring in hard copies.

The basic rules are that each student must read their work aloud to the class. Once finished, the class will discuss how well the writer met the requirements for the assignment. The writer may not speak during this discussion. The impulse to defend or clarify an idea will be great. It will also prevent active listening. Therefore, once finished with their reading, the writer will take notes on the class discussion, and do nothing else.

Appendix B

Following are the steps for a successful writing workshop:

1. Call the student to the front of the room and have them sit at the desk. Put the first page of their writing on a document camera or, if in electronic form, post their Page 1 on the screen. You, the teacher, will be on the opposite side of the desk, sitting with the class, and managing the feeding of the pages — either pulling the sheet of paper up the document camera or scrolling down the screen — as the writer reads their work aloud. I inform the class that the more senses we utilize, the better our comprehension. So it's important that they both see and hear the words on the page.

2. After the writer has finished reading, their sole responsibility is to take notes on the class discussion. For many students, this is a comfort. There's no need to confront the class, the writer can just put their head down and scribble away. For those who might want to defend some aspect of their work (and this tends to be the more common experience), this rule prevents their doing so and forces them to actively listen. I assure them that the words on the page must speak for themselves. If there's something the writer wishes to clarify, this must be done in the revision of the work.

3. The class should lead the discussion with gentle guidance from you. Be sure they stay focused on the assignment. This is not a Literature course so there should be no analyzing of the story — only if and how the elements of the assignment are incorporated.

4. When the students revise and submit their work, they should include the notes from that assignment's workshop. This will allow you to see how they incorporated the feedback from the discussion into their revision.

A benefit of conducting a workshop of this nature is that it fosters a trust and intimacy among the students. They get to know each other's style, and learn to recognize each other's voice. They witness the progress and shifts of their classmates' developing craft. It is one of the most rewarding aspects of the workshop — for the students and for you, the teacher.

For the independent writer, who's not in a classroom, you will want to approximate this important workshop. To do so, consider reading your work to a group of people who you trust to be honest and constructively critical, letting them know your goal for each individual piece.

You will follow the same strategy as outlined above:

- Give your group the rules of the assignment — particularly that they are to read for the implementation of the required elements and not conduct an analysis of the narrative.

- Read your work aloud, ideally in a way that your group can follow along visually — either shared on a screen or printed out on paper and given to each participant.

- Take notes on their discussion without participating in the conversation.

- Consider their feedback when revising the work.

- Repeat.

APPENDIX C

Pre-Writing Outline Template

I. Main character:
   A. Name
   B. Description
   C. 10-15 questions about the main character, for example: How would you describe your personality? Did you enjoy high school? Why or why not? Who do you miss most? Why? etc.

II. Secondary character:
   A. Name
   B. Description
   C. 10-15 questions
      1. What do you think of school so far?
      2. Do you have a lot of friends or a close few?
      3. What do you like most about the main character?
      4. Etc.

III. Setting
   A. Where we are
   B. How this affects your main character

IV. Anticipated Quest and Conflict
   A. What your character seeks
      1. E.g., A date with the girl in his class
   B. Obstructions he encounters
      1. E.g., Too shy to walk right up to her
      2. E.g., None of his friends seem to know her

V. Anticipated change for main character

VI. Why your readers should care about your main character

VII. Your reason for writing this story

WORKS CITED

Baldwin, Amy. "Re: Guidelines for Short Fiction." Received by Jennifer Gessner. 14 Mar 2020.

Bounds, Gwendolyn. "How Handwriting Trains the Brain." *Wall Street Journal* 5 Oct 2015.

Chopin, Kate. "The Story of an Hour." *St. Louis Life* 5 January 1895.

Holtz, Robert Lee. "Can Handwriting Make You Smarter?" *Wall Street Journal* 14 April 2016.

James, Karin H. "The Importance of Handwriting Experience on the Development of the Literate Brain." *Current Directions in Psychological Science*, vol 26, issue 6, 2017.

Marquez, Gabriel Garcia. "One of These Days." *No One Writes to the Colonel: and Other Stories,* Harper & Row, Publishers, Inc. 1968, pp 73-76.

Marquez, Gabriel Garcia. *100 Years of Solitude.* Translated by Gregory Rabassa, Penguin Classics, 2000.

Martinez, Esteban. Writer, Lawyer and Former Professor.

O'Connor, Flannery. "Good Country People." *A Good Man is Hard to Find and Other Stories.* Harcourt, Brace & Company, 1955.

Salinger, J.D. *The Catcher in the Rye.* Little, Brown and Company, 1951.

Tallent, Elizabeth. "No One's a Mystery." *Harper's,* August 1985, pp 28-29.

Watson, P. "What People Usually Fear." *The Sunday Times* [London] 7 October 1973, p. 9.

ABOUT THE AUTHOR

Jennifer Gessner believes everyone has a story (or many) to tell, and she loves to help aspiring authors learn how to develop and share theirs. Gessner's extensive experience as a development editor at a major publisher and as a college writing professor gives her the unique vantage point to understand what is compelling to both publishers and readers alike. Gessner has the clear conviction that writing is a skill that can be taught — just like playing a musical instrument or serving an ace on the tennis court.

During her professional career, Gessner won the coveted honor of developing "Book of the Year," was one of the principal editors of an award-winning student literary magazine, and helped to establish the Creative Writing program at her college.

Her bio includes:

Teacher of Writing
- Hudson Valley Writers Center
- SUNY - Westchester Community College
- Community College of Denver
- University of Colorado, Denver

Development Editor
- OpenStax at Rice University
- Pearson

Independent Writing Coach

Jenny now works with authors to help them develop their books — from honing their skills as a writer, to developing their book plan, to getting their manuscript started, to refining their completed manuscript into an agent-ready product.

And, of course, she still teaches writing, which is what she loves most and what she hopes to do for you through this book.

For speaking engagements, to schedule a writers' workshop, or to receive manuscript support from Frontlist Editorial Services, please write to: jennifergessner@frontlisteditorial.com.

www.ingramcontent.com/pod-product-compliance
Lightning Source LLC
Chambersburg PA
CBHW061234070526
44584CB00030B/4118